KU-574-662

MORE
WAYS TO HANDLE
GROWN-UPS

Also in Beaver by Jim and Duncan Eldridge

How To Handle Grown-Ups
What Grown-Ups Say and What They Really Mean
Bogeys, Boils and Belly Buttons

And by Jim Eldridge

The Wobbly Jelly Joke Book

MORE WAYS TO HANDLE GROWN-UPS

Jim and Duncan Eldridge

Illustrated by
David Mostyn

Beaver Books

A Beaver Book
Published by Arrow Books Limited
62–5 Chandos Place, London WC2N 4NW

An imprint of Century Hutchinson Ltd

London Melbourne Sydney Auckland
Johannesburg and agencies throughout the world

First published 1987

Set in Century Schoolbook
by JH Graphics Ltd, Reading

Made and printed in Great Britain
by Anchor Brendon Ltd
Tiptree, Essex

ISBN 0 09 951310 2

INTRODUCTION

Our first two books, *How To Handle Grown-Ups*, and *What Grown-Ups Say And What They Really Mean*, were mainly concerned with advice on how to handle your grown-ups in your own home, or at school.

However, we were deluged with letters from children saying that their problem was not at home – where they could always hide somewhere safe (like in their own room) – but when their grown-ups took them out somewhere.

We saw at once that there was a need for a book to advise young people on how to get their own way with grown-ups when *away* from home. The real need was to make sure that grown-ups were stopped from taking their children to places they didn't want to go (e.g. visiting boring relatives, being dragged around art galleries, or being made to be a bridesmaid or a page at a wedding).

In this book you will find plenty of ways to make sure that you will never again be invited out to any of these awful occasions. So, here it is: How Not To Get Invited Back, or *More Ways to Handle Grown-Ups: Out and About.*

The best of luck with your grown-ups!

Jim and Duncan Eldridge

How to MAKE SURE YOU ARE NOT INVITED BACK TO THE home of BORING RELATIVES And Friends of your PARENTS

For some strange reason parents insist on taking their children to visit relatives and friends of theirs who are among the most boring people the human race has ever produced. What is worse, parents insist during these visits that their children: (a) dress in 'smart' uncomfortable clothes; (b) remain silent during the visit, with only the occasional spot of quiet breathing allowed.

It has always struck us that this is a perfect example of the hypocrisy of parents. They spend years teaching their children to walk and talk, and as soon as they can they tell them: 'Sit down and keep quiet.'

Why do they insist on their children accompanying them on these awful visits? When their child complains, parents say, 'If you don't shut up we'll leave you here and go without you.' When the child says, 'Good, that's what I want,' the parents ignore this remark and force their offspring into hideous clothes, bundle them into the nearest form of transport, and force them to endure mind-numbing boredom for what seems like two eternities.

Well this is how to get out of it. This is how to make sure that after one visit you are never invited back again.

A. Break Things

Aim for something irreplaceable, like an heirloom that has been in the family for generations. If there are none lying around, go for something expensive. But remember to apologize afterwards ('I'm so sorry, I didn't realize it was there.'). This will make it impossible for the awful relative/friend to ask you or your parents to pay for it. (On the other hand, if your parents have to pay for it, it serves the same purpose: they won't let you go back.)

Some useful targets are:

chairs
cups
saucers
plates
ornaments
floorboards
bannisters
records: however, first make sure that any record you smash is one of the grown-ups'

favourites. If you 'accidentally' break, bend, warp or sit on a record that one of them has always hated, but been afraid to get rid of because the other one's mother gave it to them as a present, then this will defeat your object. You will be invited back, taken on tours through the house and given all the things they hate to look at (e.g. book-ends from Uncle Arthur).

There are plenty of things that you can dismantle with one sharp pull. For all of them

you can use the same excuse, 'It came off in my hand.' Useful targets include:
    door handles
    door bells
    toilet cistern handles
    toilet-roll holders
    handles of cups
    the whiskers of ornamental animals.

B. Ruin Furniture

Stick the following on your hosts' furniture:
    food
    vomit
    snot
    chewing gum
    nose pickings
    drink (preferably something sticky)
    dirty soles of shoes.

Drop any of the above on to cloth-covered furniture, curtains or carpets. (*Note:* It's a waste of time dropping/sticking them on shiny wood, metal or plastic furniture. The marks can be wiped off too easily.)

Once your chosen substance hits the material (carpet, chair cover, or whatever), smear it in to make it permanent.

C. Food

Eat disgustingly: keep your mouth open at all times, and make sure it is always crammed to overflowing so that food falls out as you eat.

Talk as you eat: spray food with every word. Talk to lots of people while eating, it sprays the food in more directions.

Choke on food: go purple in the face, clutch your throat and fall on the floor, moaning, 'I've been poisoned!'

Don't eat any of the food. This always offends someone who has spent hours preparing it.

Pull funny faces as you eat to let everyone know you think the food is horrible.

Put other people off their food by talking about disgusting subjects at meal-times (e.g. nose pickings, diseases involving open wounds, what goes into a sausage).

SUDDENLY FEELING ODD

Peer at the food carefully, then pick something out, examine it, and say, 'There's a mouse dropping in this.' Then eat it.

Put lots of *tomato ketchup* on everything.

Say things like:

'The food's not as bad as Mum/Dad said it would be.'

'Mum/Dad said you wouldn't give us much to eat.'

'Luckily we ate before we came.'

'I suppose lots of people like this kind of thing.'

'Did you know this sort of food is bad for you?'

'I'm sure I saw something move on my plate.'

D. Criticize the House

Direct

'Don't you ever clean the house?'

'What's that terrible smell? Doesn't your toilet work?'

'Your windows need washing. Do you leave them until it rains?'

'These chairs look a bit cheap.'

'What awful wallpaper.'

'Is this house due to be demolished?'

'This table's got woodworm.'

'Look, that's a rat dropping. I recognize it because we're studying rats in biology.'

'Aren't your floors filthy.'

'Do we have to drink out of these cups?'

Subtle

'Weren't these the chairs that were reported stolen on *Police 5*?'

'I don't think this house is as big a mess as Mum and Dad said it was.'

'I know the name of a window cleaner if you want one.'

'I'm sure this house will look very nice when it's finished.'

'I shouldn't worry what other people say about your house, so long as you like it, that's all that matters.'

'Was this furniture here when you moved in, or did the dustmen deliver it by mistake?'

'Are you against using cleaning materials for environmental reasons?'

'I suppose after a while you build up an immunity to germs and dirt.'

'I expect it must be lots of fun to get your furniture from jumble sales.'

'Isn't it amazing how quickly a house gets dirty?'

'Has your vacuum cleaner broken?'

'I don't care what other people say, *I* think your house looks . . . all right.'

E. Indulge in Embarrassing Topics of Conversation

'My grandfather suffers from piles. He has to sit on a rubber cushion with a hole in it.'

'Our cat's got diarrhoea.'

'I hear your aunt's in prison.'

'I thought we might have to eat out of a trough because Mum says you eat like pigs here.'

'They found head lice at our school last week, and now I feel all itchy.'

'I hear you're very poor.'

'Is that really a wig?'

'How does a fish drink? I only ask because Dad says you drink like one and I've never seen it before.'

'I hear that you voted for (*their favourite political party*). My Dad says he always wondered what sort of people voted for them.'

'Our dog's got fleas.'

'My Dad says unions should be banned by law from going on strike.'

'Did you cut your hair like that on purpose or did it get caught in something?'

'You're not getting a divorce after all, then?'

'My Grandad was arrested again last week.'

'What did you have electric shock treatment for?'

'This boy in our class has got this rare illness that means wax keeps oozing out of his nose.'

'I see your hair transplant wasn't very successful.'

'Was your daughter very heart-broken when her fiancé dumped her?'

'I think we ought to ban all nuclear weapons.' (*or*) 'I think nuclear weapons are a good thing.' (*This depends on the views of your hosts. Pick the one they will totally disagree with.*)

'Mum says that (*your hosts' favourite singer or group*) are rubbish.'

'Dad says that he can't understand what sort of idiot watches (*your hosts' favourite TV programme*).'

How to Avoid FURTHER VISITS to MUSEUMS AND ART GALLERIES

Grown-ups take children to museums and art galleries for two reasons:

1. *To impress the other people* in the museum or gallery with their knowledge as they spout out facts aloud to you. (e.g. 'That picture was painted by Picasso. You can tell by the sort of shapes he paints.' They forget to add that an even bigger clue to the identity of the artist is the signature in the corner.)

2. *To try to educate you.* Your argument that a comic has as much educational value as a visit to the museum is usually disregarded by adults, who all pretend that they never ever read comics when they were children but only Good Books by people like Shakespeare.

To get out of being dragged on further visits to museums or art galleries, it is worth concentrating on the above points, by:

1. Embarrassing your grown-up in front of other people.
2. Making it appear that your education has been terrible, and it's all your grown-up's fault.

The ultimate aim, of course, is to get yourself banned from these places after your first visit, then you won't be allowed back in anyway.

A. Museums

Embarrassing Things to Say in Museums

'Why have they only got old stuff here! Can't they afford new things?'

'If the Ancient Chinese were so clever why didn't they invent a fork?'

'That doesn't look like a Stone Age axe head; it looks like a lump of rock out of our garden.'

Go up to an ancient statue of a nude man (usually a god) and say loudly, 'Hasn't he got a tiny willy.'

Go up to an ancient statue of a nude woman (usually a goddess) and say, 'Her boobs aren't as big as my teacher's.'

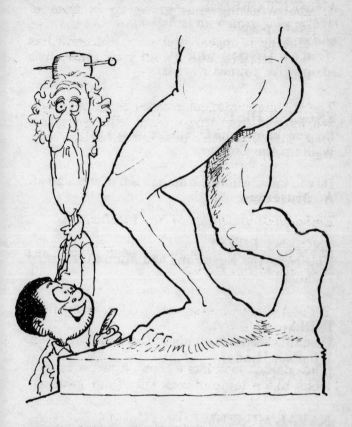

Awful Jokes to Crack in Specialist Museums, or Museum Departments

PREHISTORY
Do you know what came after the Iron Age and the Bronze Age!
The Saus-age.

ANCIENT GREECE
(When your grown-up is looking at Greek vases and urns.)
What's a Grecian urn?
About fifty pounds a week.

ENGLISH HISTORY
Do you know which King was a nut?
William the Conker.

Do you know where the Magna Carta was signed?
At the bottom.

ANCIENT EGYPT
How come the Egyptians had Mummies but no Daddies?

INDIA
I see this section's all about the Hindu religion.
What's a Hindu?
It lays eggs.

NAVAL MUSEUM
What do you get if you cross the Atlantic with the Titanic?
Halfway.

MILITARY MUSEUM
We had our electricity bill in last week. My Dad called it The Charge of the Light Brigade.

Things to Say in Each Museum Department that are Wrong and will Embarrass the Grown-up with you

PREHISTORY
'Did you know that you and I are descended from apes? Especially you.'

VIKING
'Did you know that the Vikings' boats were made of raspberry jelly so they would have something to eat if they got hungry?

ANCIENT ROME
'Did you know that an Ancient Roman invented the first ever motor car, but because no one invented petrol for another two thousand years he thought it would never work, so he dropped the idea? His name was Julius Caesar Mercedes.'

'Did you know that Roman roads were built straight because they hadn't invented the curved kerbstone to go around corners?'

ANCIENT GREECE
'Did you know that the ancient Greeks had one glass eye each?'

ANCIENT EGYPT
'Did you know that the Egyptian Empire was named after the Empire cinema in London?'

ANCIENT BRITAIN
'Did you know that Stonehenge is made of Plasticine?'

SAXON
'Did you know that the Saxons invented the saxophone?'

ENGLISH HISTORY
'Did you know that the Black Death was caused by a load of mouldy pork sausages?'

'Did you know that Henry VIII had nine wives and they were all called Jane, except for eight of them?'

'Did you know that Sir Walter Raleigh invented the bicycle?'

ANCIENT BIBLICAL WORLD
'Did you know that Alexander the Great's Dad was called Alexander the Greater? He was actually named after an ancient Egyptian cheese grater, but they couldn't spell properly in those days.'

'Did you know that the Hittites were so called because they used to hit everyone?'

'Did you know that all the coins made before Jesus Christ was born have BC after the date on them?'

SCIENCE
'Did you know that gravity wasn't invented until A D 700? Before that everyone used to float in the air, which is why no one wore shoes.'

'Did you know that the Angles invented geometry?'

AMERICA

'Did you know that Ancient Mexicans believed that if you unwound your ear your nose fell off?'

'Did you know that when Christopher Columbus discovered America he was really looking for Russia but he had his map upside down?'

FRANCE

'Did you know that Joan of Arc was Noah's wife?'

'Did you know that Louis XIV of France was known as the Sun King because he was the son of a King?

CHINA

'Did you know that the Great Wall of China was only meant to be 50 metres long, but the builders had lost the part of the plans that told them how to end it?'

'Did you know that Ghenghis Khan used to play in goal for Real Madrid?'

EXPLORERS

'Did you know that Marco Polo invented the Mars Bar 300 years ago, but it didn't become popular because no one wanted a Mars Bar with a hole in it.'

B. Art Galleries

Stand by a painting and say, 'Is this the painting they found out was a fake? Why is it still hanging here?'

Breathe on a sculpture and polish it with your sleeve.

Say in a loud voice to your grown-up, 'Are you sure we can get away with stealing this painting?'

Stick chewing gum on a sculpture.

Go up to one of the attendants (usually to be found slumped on a chair) and say, 'What's this sculpture supposed to be? It looks like a load of old clothes with a pumpkin for a head.'

Stand some distance from a famous abstract painting and say loudly, 'Is this the one you said was a load of rubbish. I see what you mean when you said it's all just a con trick. Fancy paying someone thousands of pounds just for spilling a few pots of paint.'

Look out for a modern sculpture with a hole in it, and stick your head through it. If your head gets stuck, so much the better, as they will have to call the Fire Brigade to cut the sculpture into pieces to get you out.

Find a famous portrait (e.g. the Mona Lisa) and take out a felt-tip pen as if you are about to draw a moustache on it.

Sit on a big sculpture and say, 'Gee up!'

Say, 'How much do you reckon the frame's worth? It's better than the picture.'

Say, 'If you look carefully you can see it was done by Paint-By-Numbers.'

Pretend to recognize people you know in paintings:

> 'That woman holding that swan looks just like the woman who lives next door. She doesn't wear many clothes either, does she, Dad?'

> 'That man having his head chopped off looks just like my teacher.'

> 'The dog in that picture is like the one that lives next door to the greengrocer. Remember, it did a wee up against our front door.'

> 'See the ant in that picture? My friend had one just like that in a matchbox.'

Make jokes about, or mispronounce, the names of famous artists as you look at the paintings:

Constable: 'Fancy a policeman painting pictures like that.'
or
If that's the best he could paint, no wonder he never got promoted to Sergeant.'

Picasso: Pronounce it 'Pickaxe-o'.

Whistler: Say the name, give a whistle, then laugh at your own joke.

Leonardo da Vinci: Pronounce it as Leonard (or Lenny) day Vinky.

Vincent van Gogh: Have lots of fun with this. Attempt to pronounce his last name as many times as possible. The record is held by a boy in Scotland who was able to mispronounce the name no less than 27 times (Goff, Goof, Guff, Gug, Gog, Golf, Go, Gowf, Gudge, etc). As a result his embarrassed father was barred from the local Art Gallery and his local Art Club.

C. Museums *and* Art Galleries

Things to Do to Embarrass your Grown-Up

Drop a load of tiny round boiled sweets on the floor. They will roll all over the place and every time someone treads on one they will crunch it underfoot. This also works well with marbles, although with marbles people tend to fall over when they tread on them.

Call out, 'Has anyone seen my pet mouse (*or snake, or rat*)? It seems to have escaped from my pocket.' This will clear the room you are in within seconds.

If there is a really large exhibition hall with a polished floor, slide across it.

Test the echo in the big rooms by shouting.

Things to Say to Embarrass your Grown-Up

'How much longer have we got to stay here?'

'Either the drains in this place don't work or someone's just made a bad smell.'

'When there was a programme about this place on the telly you turned it over to *East Enders*.'

'Aren't these places boring.'

'Don't you get some odd people in these places.'

'You said that only posers go to these places.'

'Where are the toilets in this place?'

'This place used to be a hospital for contagious diseases.'

How to Avoid BEING TAKEN BACK to VISIT PEOPLE IN HOSPITAL

For some reason grown-ups always want to take children with them when they go hospital visiting. They do this in spite of the fact that hospital authorities hate children and either ban them from the wards, or else insist that they sit on uncomfortable chairs and keep absolutely still while everyone is gathered around the bed of the patient.

Often the person you are taken to visit in hospital is an adult that you would never want to visit even when they were fit and healthy, so why grown-ups think you would want to see them when they are ill and spotty and in plaster and generally Yuk is a complete mystery. Also, the last thing an ill adult would want is a visit from someone like you. Such a visit would quite likely cause them to have a relapse.

Because of this it is in the patient's interests (as well as yours) that you do your best to get out of visiting people when they are in hospital.

The exceptions to this are:

1. People you like.

2. Rich people who might leave you something in their will.

Sooner or later your grown-ups will insist on taking you hospital visiting. It is difficult (but not impossible: see *Before You Get to the Hospital*) to get out of this very first visit. If you cannot, remember that good dodgers should be able to use this first visit to make sure that they never again have to go hospital visiting.

A. Before You Get to the Hospital

This is an important part of the strategy. Make sure that your parents know that you don't want to go hospital visiting because:

Hospitals are full of ill people, which means they are full of germs, which means you are bound to catch something.

You have a fear of hospitals which brings you out either in spots or stripes.

It is a long way and the journey will make you feel ill. (This excuse also applies to museums, art galleries, visits to relatives, etc.)

It will upset you to see your favourite aunt/uncle/granny/neighbour lying in a hospital bed.

The doctors and nurses in that hospital are horrible to children.

Children aren't allowed to go visiting in that particular hospital.

If none of these works and your hard-hearted grown-ups insist on taking you, then make the journey as difficult as you can:

> If going by train, tell them the train is on the wrong platform.
>
> If going by car or coach, keep wanting to go to the toilet, or be sick.

For further suggestions, see the Section *How To Make Sure That Your Future Journeys With Your Parents Are Shorter and Better* (page 56).

B. At the Hospital

Things to Do

The patient will be sure to have a bowl of fruit by the bed. Eat their fruit. If they have sweets, eat their sweets as well.

Make rude noises as if you are suffering from wind.

Scrape the legs of your chair on the polished floor. It makes a terrible screeching sound that will set everyone's teeth on edge.

'Accidentally' knock things over (e.g. a vase full of flowers; the patient's dinner).

Give the patient a friendly pat on whatever part of them is in plaster (e.g. broken leg, broken arm).

Fall asleep while the patient is in the middle of talking to you. Even better, lie on their bed and fall asleep.

Things to Say

'That man/woman in the next bed looks really ill. What's he/she got?'

'Do you mind if I take a photograph of you? Just in case.'

Make rude remarks about the hospital staff in stage whispers (i.e. just loud enough for it to be heard): 'I don't like the look of that doctor. He looks like the butcher who lives down our street,' and, 'Does that nurse drink? Her eyes are all bloodshot.'

'Are you going to have tubes and things sticking out of you when we come again?'

'I know someone else who was in this same ward. He died.'

'You're better off in here than outside. Outside everyone is saying terrible things about you behind your back.'

'I didn't bring you any flowers because I didn't think you'd be well enough to appreciate them, and it seemed a pity to waste the money.'

'I bought you some sweets to cheer you up, but I ate them on the way here.'

'Do they have an undertaker attached to this hospital?'

'Are you sure you don't want me to call the nurse? You look terrible.'

'The plants in your garden have all withered and died since you've been in hospital.'

'Mum says she never knew you had a clean pair of pyjamas/nightdress.'

'This is one of the filthiest hospitals I've ever seen. Didn't the Health Minister threaten to close it down last year?'

'Is your house locked up safely? They've had a lot of burglaries in your street since you've been in here.'

'I hope your operation went well, beause I read in the newspaper that this hospital's run out of blood.'

'Did you know that the majority of patients leave hospital in a worse state of health than when they went in. It's a fact.'

'Did you know that this hospital is where they train student doctors. I hope they haven't given you one of these awful new students who does everything wrong.'

'Have they had this ward disinfected after that case of plague they had in here last week?'

'Have they told you yet what you've *really* got wrong with you?'

'I looked up your symptoms in a medical book and according to that you're seriously ill.'

'I think they're giving you the wrong treatment.'

'According to a friend of mind whose Mum's a doctor, pretty soon you'll start to lose all feeling all over. Once that sets in, you've had it.'

'I overheard someone say you ought to be sent home. They reckon you're not ill at all, it's all in your mind.'

'Dad said you ought to be ashamed. He said you're taking up a bed that could be used for someone who was really ill.'

'I looked up what you've got in a medical dictionary. It's worse than you thought.'

Tell Stories of Operations and Hospital Treatments that went Wrong

'I read about this man who went into hospital for an operation on his nose. By mistake they removed his leg.'

'This woman went in for an operation on her stomach and the surgeon left his rubber glove sewn up inside her.'

'You know why surgeons wear masks, don't you? It's so that they can't identify a surgeon who does an operation wrong.'

'There was this hospital where all the patients caught food poisoning because the kitchens were in a filthy state.'

'There was a woman who went into hospital for an appendix operation. She'd heard that they got so many operations wrong that she had written all over her body: "It's my appendix you should be operating on." Even then they got it wrong.'

'Be careful what drugs they give you; some of them have terrible side effects. There was one hospital where they tested these drugs on this man, and his head turned into a cabbage.'

HOW NOT TO GET INVITED TO WEDDINGS AND Christenings

How to get out of being a Bridesmaid or a Page

Sooner or later you will be invited to be a bridesmaid or a page for someone's wedding. The word 'invited' is another example of adult hypocrisy. What it means is that you *will* do this job. If you do, it is a fate worse than death.

The trouble is, if you are successful at it once, you will be asked to do it again at the weddings of other cousins, aunts or uncles. To avoid this it is of the utmost importance that you do it all wrong the first time.

Stand on the bride's train. (This is the long part of her dress that drags along behind her.) Do it suddenly and she will fall over. Do it right from her entrance into the church and she will feel as if she is dragging a ton of coal behind her.

Trip the bridegroom up. With a bit of luck he will fall into the bride, who will crash into her father, who will fall on to the vicar, and the whole lot will tumble down like a row of falling dominoes.

36

Mumble and mutter under your breath, but just loud enough to irritate the bride and groom.

Hum a song tunelessly.

Pretend to find a ring on the church floor (use a curtain ring), and say, 'The best man must have dropped this ring.' It will cause havoc.

Use superstition. Whisper things to the bride like, 'There's a black cat over there in the church. Isn't it unlucky on your wedding day?' and, 'They said it was lucky if the bride was kissed by a chimney sweep, so I've arranged for a chimney sweep to call on you. Unfortunately he can't make it until just after midnight.'

How to get out of being a Guest at a Wedding or Christening

Although not in the same league as being a bridesmaid or page, being a guest at a wedding is still pretty awful. The same goes for being a guest at a christening. For one thing, both ceremonies are so boring. Who really wants to see a baby having its head washed, especially when you have to stand in a cold and draughty church for what seems like weeks?

Make sure that your first 'invitation' to such an event is your last.

Embarrassing Things to Say at Weddings

'You'd think she'd have done better for herself than him.' (*Or:* 'You'd think he'd have done better for himself than her.')

37

'Does he know about her other boyfriends?' (*Or:* 'Does she know about his other girlfriends?')

'Has she told him about her disease?' (*Or:* 'Has he told her about his disease?')

'I hope the food is better than at the last wedding reception I was at. It was so bad there that I ate the bride's bouquet.'

'If he's the best man then why isn't she marrying him?'

'Kiss the bride? With that face? I'd rather kiss the vicar.'

'I'm not surprised the bride's father is giving her away. He'd be lucky to find anyone who'd pay for her.'

'She always said she liked the simple things in life. Dad says now she's marrying one.'

'Mum says that the bridegroom's been left at the altar so many times he can find his way down the aisle blindfolded.'

'The bridegroom has forgotten to take the price sticker off the bottom of his shoe.'

'Look at the bride's father. His trousers are undone.'

'I wouldn't have thought the bride would have worn that colour dress, it shows up all her spots.'

'Have you ever noticed how brides always choose bridesmaids uglier than them so that they will look pretty. She must have had a tough time finding those bridesmaids.'

Awful Jokes to Crack at Weddings

(*Note:* the joke is to be said loudly, with a terrible cackling laugh at the end of it.)

Where do rabbits go when they get married? On a bunnymoon.

What do you call spiders when they get married? Newlywebs.

Did you hear about the two octopuses who got married. They walked down the aisle hand in hand, hand in hand, hand in hand, hand in hand, hand in hand, hand in hand, hand in hand, hand in hand.

Do you know how many wives a man gets when he gets married?
16. 4 better, 4 worse, 4 richer, 4 poorer.

Embarrassing Things to Say at Christenings

'What an ugly baby. Who do you reckon he takes after?'

'Why is the vicar putting water on it? Didn't they wash it before they brought it here?'

'Are you sure it's a baby? I'm sure I've seen similar things in the zoo.'

'Either that baby's uglier than I thought, or the vicar's holding it the wrong way up.'

'If that man's the baby's godfather, does that mean he's in the Mafia?'

'I bet the vicar drops the baby in the font.'

'I think the baby's just filled its nappy.'

'Why have we come here? You said you didn't believe in christenings.'

Awful Jokes to Crack at Christenings

(*Note:* as with the awful jokes at weddings, tell them in a loud voice, and add a terrible cackling laugh at the end.)

My friend was christened Glug Glug. The vicar fell in the font.

Do you know how a baby plays football?
By dribbling.

When the Czar of Russia and his wife, the Czarina, had twins, do you know what they were called?
Czardines.

Do you know where baby apes sleep?
In apricots.

Why is a baby like our old car?
Because they've both got a rattle.

Dad said their baby was born at home, but after his Mum saw it she had to be taken to hospital.

Embarrassing Things that can be Said either at Weddings or Christenings

'Can't they afford heating in this place?'

'Why is that priest wearing a dress?'

'Look at those numbers in that frame on the wall.' (*Note:* these are the numbers of the hymns.) 'They're just like the numbers of the winning horses when you take me to the betting shop.'

'These seats are so hard my bum's getting sore.'

'How long have we got to keep kneeling? My leg's going stiff.'

'When do we eat?'

'Is this the place where you said you once practised Black Magic?'

'Do they have a collection? Is that how the vicar gets his wages?'

'Dad, have you told Mum how you got thrown out of the church choir when you were my age?'

41

Embarrassing Things to Do at Weddings or Christenings

Talk all the time. When people say 'Shh' to you, look around to see who they are shushing.

Sing very loudly and out of tune when everyone sings the hymns. Even better, sing a different hymn from everyone else.

Start to scratch. This will irritate the people around you. Say to them apologetically: 'I'm sorry, but I've got fleas.' They will then start to scratch as well.

Yawn. This is very catching. Soon everyone in the church will be yawning. With a bit of luck they will all fall asleep.

How Best to OFfEND PEOPLE with YOUR CLOTHING

This is very important. Badly dressed children are not welcome in other people's houses. So, the worse dressed you are, the less welcome you will be.

Here are a few examples of just how badly you can dress:

Messy
Just before entering anywhere you wish to be thrown out of, roll in mud. Usually wherever there is mud there are trees with loads of leaves lying under them. When you are covered in mud, roll in the leaves. When you stand up you will resemble a bush. Now go in.

Food-stained
Spread as much food over your clothes and your face, hair and hands as you can. Give the appearance of having eaten out of a trough blindfolded, using a shovel.

Torn
Tear off a sleeve. Split the seams of your clothing. Pull out the stuffing from any padded clothes. Make it look as if you were caught up in a lawn mower.

Garish

Wear the most hideous and brightly decorated clothes that you can find. Mix combinations in the worst possible taste. Dye your hair bright colours. Paint your face. Wear loads of flashing ornaments.

Punk

Although now pretty outdated, this style is still calculated to drive most adults into a fury. Wear shredded clothes, and T-shirts and jackets with rude slogans on them. Shave half the hair off your head. Pin your clothes together with as many safety pins as you can bear the weight of without falling over.

Smelly
Similar to Messy, except instead of mud, find a
dung heap to roll about in. Put a few dead fish
in your pockets. Smear dog mess on the soles of
your shoes.

Paper Bag over the Head
Find a large paper bag, cut out two holes for
your eyes, and put it over your head. This
always makes grown-ups worry: what is under
the paper bag?

Nude
(Although the chances of you actually getting anywhere in this outfit are very small.)

How to Get out of Going ~~Anywhere~~ Anywhere

The basic rule here is to pretend to be ill. How ill you pretend to be depends on where your parents plan to take you, and how long you want to be thought of as 'ill'. Remember, if you pretend to have bubonic plague one day, do not be surprised if your parents get suspicious if you say you are all right the next morning to go to a party.

The best illnesses to fake are the following:

Measles, etc. (anything with spots)
Use a felt tip pen to put spots on your face. Make sure you use the correct colour (e.g. reddish-brown). Green spots are very suspicious and might make your grown-up think you are a visitor from another planet.

Sprained Ankle
Limp and go 'ouch' every now and then. Lean heavily on furniture and other objects as you walk along.

Sprained Arm or Shoulder
Clutch your arm to your side and wince and moan a lot. Tell everyone that you are unable to write.

Colds and Flu

Squirt water up your nose so that it keeps running down. Spread vaseline around your nostrils to make your nose look wet and shiny. If you are given a thermometer to take your temperature, put it on a radiator or a hot water bottle first.

Vomiting

Rub flour or a white cream on to your face to give you a very pale appearance. When you go into the toilet, leave the door open so that the retching noises you make can be clearly heard by your grown-ups.

Diarrhoea
We will not go into nasty details here. Just keep going into the toilet a lot, and stay there for ages and ages.

Stomach Ache
Bend over, clutch your stomach, moan, groan and writhe in agony. Complain of pains that are 'like a knife'.

Concussion
First you need to tell your grown-ups that you banged your head earlier. *(Note*: you do not actually have to have banged your head, just tell them you did.) Once they know that you have been injured in this way, wander about in a dazed manner, with a glazed look in your eyes. Mutter things like 'Where am I?' and 'Who are you?' Walk into walls.

How to MAKE sure that future Journeys with your PARENTS ARE SHORTER AND BETTER

The aim of these dodges is to ensure that any journey you have to make with your grown-ups is as short and as pleasant as possible.

The rules here are:-

1. If the first journey is by cramped coach, make sure that the journey is so awful that in future they will travel by train (First Class, naturally, in order to keep you away from people); or by car (a large roomy comfortable car, of course).

2. If the journey is a really long one, persuade them to take a plane.

Here's how to do it:

While Waiting for the Coach or Train

Keep your grown-ups in a state of nervousness by calling out, 'That looks like our one!' every few minutes.

Keep saying, 'Are you sure this is the right stop (*or* platform)?'

Say, 'I just overheard someone say the drivers are on strike.'

Complain about the cold weather, even if it is boiling hot.

Hide any luggage. This will drive your grown-ups into a panic.

Go to the toilet, and wait until the coach or train arrives before re-appearing.

On the Coach or Train

Keep asking to use the toilet.

Keep telling your grown-up (in a loud voice) that you feel sick.

Complain that there is nowhere for you to stretch out.

Go for walks up and down the aisles 'to stretch my legs, otherwise I'll get cramp.' As you walk, tread on people's feet and trip over their luggage.

Go up to strangers and say, 'Would you like to see my pet cockroach.'

Find a passenger who wants to be left in peace to read a book, and start talking to them.

Open the windows and freeze everyone.

Sit next to someone and pretend to fall asleep.
Let your head rest on their shoulder. Snore.
Dribble on their clothing.

Tell the other passengers that you have an
infectious disease.

Pretend to search for your missing mouse (or
lizard, or some other small animal).

This one needs preparation beforehand. Get a
polythene bag and put vegetable salad in mayon-

naise into it. In the middle of your journey suddenly say, 'Urgh! I feel sick!' Pick up the polythene bag (carefully concealing its contents), put your head into it, and pretend to be sick. Then take out a spoon and start to eat the mayonnaise salad.

Let off stink bombs.

Blow bubbles all over the other passengers.

Keep asking for things to be handed down to you from the luggage rack, and then put back up again.

Make loud comments to your grown-ups about the other passengers. ('Hasn't that man got a big nose'; 'Look at that terrible dress that woman's wearing', etc.)

Ask to borrow another passenger's newspaper. Then:
(a) Tear it up, telling them you are practising to be a magician. Look sorry when your 'trick' doesn't work and the newspaper remains torn into bits.
or
(b) Blow your nose into it, telling them that you have run out of paper handkerchiefs.

Tell stories about terrible coach or train disasters. ('There was this terrible train crash only last month. A train came off the rails and everyone was killed'; 'Did you hear about the coach that crashed on this motorway last year?

Terrible. Everyone died. It was owned by the same firm as this coach. That's a coincidence, isn't it?' etc.)

In a Car

1. Complaints about your Grown-Up's Driving

'You're driving too fast.'

'You're driving too slow.'

'You're too close to that car in front.'

'You should have turned left/right back there.'

'You shouldn't hold the steering wheel like that'

'Why not let Mum/Dad drive?'

'You're not sitting properly the way a good driver does.'

'You're in the wrong lane.'

'Shouldn't you have sounded your horn round that bend?'

'What colour was that traffic light we just went through? I'm sure it was red.'

'You went a bit close when you overtook that car just then'

'Don't you think it's unfair on us to drive so dangerously?'

2. General Off-Putting Comments

'Why is that lorry behind us flashing its lights at you?'

'Are you sure this is the right road?'

'Watch out, there's a police car ahead.'

'What's the time?' (To be asked at five-minute intervals.)

'Did you see what that sign said back there?'

'I think that wobbling noise is coming from one of our tyres.'

'Did you see that rare bird that nearly hit us?'

'You've just run over a hedgehog.'

'The man in that car that overtook us just now was waving at you and pointing. I wonder what he was trying to tell us?'

'My friend's family have got a much better car than ours.'

'Isn't that the wrong indicator you're using?'

'This car door's loose.'

'Was that a parking space back there?'

'What's that red light on the dashboard that keeps coming on?'

'I hope we don't get a puncture. I can't remember if I put the jack back in when I put all that stuff in the boot.'

'Careful how you reverse, I think there's a little post just behind you.'

'I think that sign said there's a hidden entrance for lorries just along this road.'

'I said we should have gone the other way.'

On an Aeroplane

It is advisable not to try any funny business on a plane because the pilot might get fed up with you and have you thrown out, or force you to ride on the wing.

How to get out of Going for Walks

For some odd reason grown-ups are obsessed with the practice of 'going for a walk'. This usually means one of two things:

A. The Country Ramble

This is a ten-mile hike across moorland and up and down mountains. It is the sort of activity that the SAS do as part of their training.

If it's not that kind of walk, it will be an equally long route march along narrow winding country lanes, and the only things you ever see are hedges two yards high. Now and then your grown-up will point out a tree to you. On these walks you are in constant danger of being run over by a tractor driven by a farmer on the lookout for walkers.

B. The City Stroll

This is a killer. It is usually a 'sight-seeing tour' in which your grown-up keeps stopping to point at buildings, and say things to you like, 'George Bernard Shaw lived there.' The fact that you haven't got the faintest idea who or what George Bernard Shaw is (or was) is brushed aside by your grown-up as he/she drags you along to another equally uninteresting building and tells you something equally boring about it.

The only thing you will get out of one of these so-called 'strolls' is sore feet from tramping on the hard pavements.

For the sake of your health both these sorts of 'walk' are to be avoided at all costs. Make sure that your first such trip is your last. Here's how to do it:

Annoying Things to Say on a Country Ramble

'I'm allergic to trees/grass/flowers/wheat/bird noises, etc.'

'The pollen in country air gives me hay fever.'

'I don't like to see how modern civilization is destroying the countryside.'

'I think the countryside ought to be dug up and concreted over.'

'I think the countryside is boring.'

'There's no fresh air out in the countryside, it always stinks of manure.'

'Aren't we trespassing?'

'Why is that angry farmer shouting at us?'

'I heard that someone was murdered around here and their ghost still haunts this place.'

'I thought I saw a sign back there saying, "Beware of the Bull". It must be hiding behind that big hedge.'

'That looks like quicksand up ahead.'

'You've just trod in the most enormous cowpat.'

'I think a bird's dropped something on your hair.'

Annoying Things to Say on a City Stroll

'Can't we afford to catch a bus?'

'Is there an amusement arcade around here?'

'Are we lost? We seem to be walking around these streets in circles.'

'Mind that lamp-post.'

'There's a policeman following us. I reckon he thinks we're up to something with all this walking around looking at buildings. I bet he thinks we're planning a robbery.'

'This city is full of muggers and robbers just waiting to jump out and attack us.'

'I read in the paper that there's going to be a demonstration march through these streets. The police say they're expecting violence. I think we ought to go home before the trouble starts.'

'Have you seen the huge amounts of dog mess all over the place?'

'Do you know that this area holds the record for the most people run over by cars and buses. I don't think we ought to cross any roads.'

'Please buy me that toy/outfit/camera, etc in that shop window over there.'

Annoying Things to Say that can be used on Both Country and City Walks

'I'm tired.'

'My leg hurts.'

'I've got a blister on my foot.'

'These shoes are too tight for me to walk properly.'

'These shoes are too loose and I keep falling over.'

'My shoelace has come undone again.'

'How much further have we got to walk? This is really boring.'

'Were your parents cruel to you, dragging you around like this?'

'I've got a cold coming on. I should be at home in the warm. This trudging around in this cold air will turn it into pneumonia.'

'It's going to rain.'

'I'm hungry.'

'You'll have to go on without me, I can't make it. But don't worry, I'll be all right.'

'I heard on the news that this is an earthquake zone, and they said that there's due to be an earthquake here today.'

'I'm sure I saw something fall out of your pocket back there.'

'Mum/Dad says you shouldn't be going for long walks in your bad condition of health.'

Persistently ask, 'How far is it?' every few minutes.

THE DIARY ~~OR~~ OF X
PRESENTS

MORE WAYS TO HANDLE GROWN UPS

Yes, folks, it's me, 'X' again. After the extracts from my diaries in *How to Handle Grown-Ups* and *What Grown-Ups Say and What They Really Mean*, in which I showed how successful I was at handling grown-ups, I thought you might like to hear about the time I had real problems with another dodger, my cousin Tracy.

Tracy is a rat and a louse and a snake and every other form of animal life I can think of. She is rotten to the core. She is also only ten years old, which should make the Universe shudder at what she will be like when she gets older.

In my opinion she is a real danger, not only to grown-ups, but to the whole human race (and any other species that happen to be about at the time). Anyway, you'll soon see for yourselves when you read these further adventures from:-

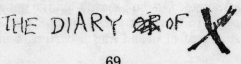

THE DIARY ~~OR~~ OF X

Saturday 26th July

Today the school holidays start, and what a piece of really dud news I've been given to start them with: this year we are not going away anywhere because we can't afford it.

'Why can't we afford it?' I asked, and back came all these excuses: inflation, the bank rate, Dad's working hours have been cut, etc, etc. In my opinion this is all a load of old rubbish. The truth is they don't want the hassle of going away. Everyone else I know is going away: Africa, Ibiza, America, France, Cornwall, Scotland. Where am I going? Nowhere! Well I think it's rotten. After the hard year I've had at school, working my skin off to get out of everything (lessons, team games, homework) I deserve a holiday.

The only good thing about it is that my Dad and Mum will feel guilty about not taking me away, so I'll be able to play on this guilt and get them to buy me things to make up for it. Maybe if I keep asking for really expensive things they'll have second thoughts and decide it's cheaper for us all to go away on holiday.

Monday 28th July

Today Mum gave me a shopping list and a ten pound note and said that I could buy myself a present with the change. (See, I knew they'd feel guilty.)

What I did was: I bought myself the present first: some new brake levers for my bike. They cost £9 something, so I wasn't able to get all the shopping. In fact I only had enough money left to buy a loaf of bread and a carton of milk.

Mum was furious and said that I should have got the shopping *first*. Anyway, two problems solved in one go: (1) I don't think I'll be sent shopping for a while; and (2) I got the new brake levers I wanted.

Tuesday 29th July
Terrible News!

As if it wasn't bad enough that we're not going anywhere for a holiday, today Mum dropped a real bombshell on me: 'Because we felt guilty about not taking you away we've invited your cousin Tracy to stay with us for ten days. We felt you could do with some company of your own age to cheer you up.'

71

Well, I was aghast. Cheer me up?! For one thing she is not my own age, she is three years younger than me. For another thing she is horrible, a blot upon the whole human race. To land her on me for ten days is on a par with giving me boils.

'Tracy is horrible,' I pointed out. 'She is rotten.'

'But she likes being with you,' said Mum.

'Only because she hopes I'm going to catch some disease off her,' I said. 'She gave me measles once, remember?'

'She didn't do it on purpose,' said Mum.

'I bet she did,' I countered. 'It's the sort of thing she would do. What about the last time I saw her, when we went to visit her family last Christmas. She was sick all over me.'

'That was an accident.'

'Oh no it wasn't. She aimed it at me.'

Unfortunately, no matter how hard I tried, Mum didn't believe me. Just because Tracy wears pink dresses with frills and has got the sort of face that baby angels wear on the tops of Christmas trees, Mum is convinced she is Miss Wonderful. I know better.

Actually I'm not completely convinced that Mum didn't invite Tracy here as an act of revenge over the case of the shopping and the brake levers.

I will just have to be on my guard while she's here. Any suggestions of sickness or disease on her part and I shall move in with the people next door.

Wednesday 30th July
Tracy arrived today. It's seven months since I

last saw her (the famous Christmas vomit incident), and she hasn't improved. She still looks like a ten-year-old-angel in frilly frocks with golden hair, but this is only to fool grown-ups. Underneath she is rotten. That Christmas (the vomit one) she had treble helpings of everything by stealing food from other people's plates, and then she blamed me for it. The child is not to be trusted.

Her arrival was sickening, with her parents giving her kisses and cuddles of goodbye, and my parents giving her kisses and cuddles of hello. I hoped that with all this cuddling she'd be squashed flat and have to be taken back home, but no such luck.

Anyway, as soon as she was in, I was off. I feel safer away from wherever this blot is, and I intend to stay safe while she is here.

Thursday 31st July
Nothing much happened today. With this human fairy doll drifting around our house, I spent most of the day out on my bike.

I worked one good dodge. I put an old and bent back wheel on my bike, and then went down to the big car park. I waited until I saw someone whose rear window was all misted up start to reverse, and I stuck my bike with the bent wheel near one of his back wheels. Just as the car started to reverse, I yelled in 'pain', banged his car, and lay down on the ground.

The car screeched to a sudden stop and the bloke got out, a really worried look on his face. He looked even more worried when he saw the bent back wheel of the bike. I didn't even need to say anything, he immediately opened his wallet and thrust four five pound notes into my hand. When I looked doubtful, he hastily added another fiver to them. He kept apologizing to me while he got back in his car and drove off.

I worked the same con in another car park a bit later on, but I only got fifteen quid that time. Still, not bad for a day's work. I decided that twice was enough because more would have been greedy, and greed is the downfall of too many dodgers.

After that I went home and had tea, and kept clear of Tracy.

I also got out of doing the washing-up after tea by saying, 'I'd love to do it, Mum, but I've got an infection under my fingernail and the washing-up liquid will only make it worse. I'm also afraid that the germs from it will breed in the hot water and infect all the plates and cups and things as I wash them up.'

All in all, a pretty successful day.

Friday 1st August
Mum tried to get me to help prepare the dinner today. I 'accidently' let the water the vegetables were cooking in boil away, and they burnt and stuck to the saucepan like lumps of charcoal. The saucepan also got burnt and had to be thrown away. There was therefore no cooked dinner for Dad, Mum, Tracy and me. Luckily I had stashed away some food in my room, so I was all right. The others had to make do with sandwiches.

I think that will put an end to my being forced to do any cooking.

As a punishment for burning the dinner, I was made to vacuum clean the house, but I soon sorted that one out. I switched the cleaner to 'blow' instead of 'suck', and it chucked great clouds of grey dust all over the living room.

Another one to me.

Later:

After having written the above diary entry I was in my room, quietly minding my own business and reading my BMX magazine, when my door opened and Tracy appeared. Luckily I had hidden all traces of my secret food store. However, it wasn't food she was after.

'You're pretty good,' she said.

I was immediately suspicious.

'What at?' I asked.

'The way you get your parents to do whatever you want.'

I gave a little smirk (after all, every genius likes their talent to be recognized), and then I wiped it off my face. What was she up to?

'I don't know what you mean,' I said.

'Yes you do,' she said. 'But I'm better.'

I let this sink in.

'Better?' I asked. 'Better at what?'

'At dodging. I can get away with more than you can.'

'Sez you,' I scoffed.

'I bet I can.'

'I bet you can't.'

'How much do you bet?'

This made me stop and think a bit. Was Tracy trying to con me? Then I thought: what am I scared of? In fact there isn't much Tracy can do to con me if I take on this bet. For one thing, I am the best dodger out and it is unthinkable that Tracy could beat me. For another thing, I could always dodge on the bet and not pay up if she tries to cheat me.

I was also on my home ground, so I had a definite advantage. Without doubt, I thought, this girl must have at least a couple of screws loose even to think of challenging me on my home territory where I know everyone's weak points (essential to the art of handling grown-ups).

'All right,' I said. 'It's a bet.'

'There's one problem,' she said. 'How are we going to score points?'

I thought about it for a bit, then I said, 'Let's score on them trying to get us to go out to rotten places.'

'Why?' asked Tracy.

'Because as you're visiting they're bound to want to take us on long boring walks to show you the sights, and to visit all your relatives who live around here.'

'But that isn't fair,' she said. 'That sort of thing will only be aimed at me.'

(Curses, I thought, this girl is smarter than I thought. That had been the whole purpose of my suggesting it.)

'I'll tell you what,' she said; 'it only counts if both of us have been included in whatever visits they've got planned.'

That seemed all right with me (although not as favourable to me as my original suggestion).

'OK,' I said. 'Now, what are we betting?'

'My favourite toy against yours.'

'No fear,' I said. 'I'm not falling for that one. You pick out some terrible knitting kit that you've never used and tell me it's your favourite. I've used that one myself. No, there's only one thing worth betting: money.'

'But I haven't got any,' she said.

'You must have. Didn't your parents give you any spending money?'

'Only a few pounds.'

Which suggested to me that she was loaded, but intending to hang on to it all the time she was with us.

'All right,' I said. 'Five pounds each.'

I saw the cash register in her head click, and then she said: 'OK. Five pounds. But how do I know I can trust you to pay up if you lose?'

I must admit that more or less the same thought had occurred to me – how I was to get the money out of Tracy when she lost.

'Tell you what,' I said. 'We'll each put five pounds into an envelope, and give the envelope to someone to hold.'

'Your parents?' she suggested.

'No,' I said.

Frankly I wouldn't trust Dad and Mum with my money. It they were as broke as they said, they'd go out and spend it.

'The man in the corner shop,' I said. 'Old Mr Carstairs.'

'Can we trust him?'

'As much as we can trust anyone.'

I nearly added, more than I can trust you. Tracy was obviously not going to be very easy to con.

'All right,' she said. 'But we've got to tell him that he only gives the envelope back to the one who's got a note signed by both of us saying to hand it over.'

'But say I win and you don't sign the note?' I pointed out.

'Then I won't get my five pounds back either,' she said. Which was a good point. So we both produced our five pound notes and put them in an envelope.

'One more rule,' she said.

'What?' I said.

'Only boring places count. If we get taken to somewhere good like a film we both want to see, that's all right.'

'Agreed,' I said.

So the contest is on. This is going to be an easy five pounds for me. I think I can say that I am quietly confident.

Saturday 2nd August

First round today.

The first thing we did was give the envelope to Mr Carstairs at the corner shop. Then the contest started in earnest.

This morning Dad and Mum announced that they'd arranged for us all to visit the local museum today. This visit would have been one of the great non-events of the century. Our local museum has to be seen to be believed: it has two bits of broken pottery, which are claimed to be Roman remains, although they look suspiciously like one of our old flowerpots; an alleged Stone Age axe head which looks like any old lump of rock; and a signed photograph of Mahatma Gandhi, who came to our town once. I expect he got off the train at the wrong station – that's the only reason I can think of for anyone famous ever coming here. In short, our local museum gives a new meaning to the word 'boring'. So I set to work. Into the toilet, lots of retching sounds, lots of time spent shut in the toilet, and loads of staggering around clutching my stomach, a victim of sickness and diarrhoea.

'I daren't go with you,' I said. 'I daren't go too far from a toilet.'

Mum and Dad were suspicious, but I felt they were also a bit relieved not to have to endure dragging me around the museum and making caustic remarks, so they nodded and said, 'Right.

You'd better stay here. But you won't mind if we take Tracy?'

'Not at all,' I said. 'I think she'd be fascinated by it.'

At this Tracy put on a sorrowful face and said, 'Oh no, I couldn't possibly go. Not when he's so ill. I know it sounds funny, Uncle and Aunt, but would you mind if we waited until he's feeling better? If we went today I wouldn't enjoy it at all, I'd just worry all the time about him being ill and all alone here.'

'He can manage,' said Mum (a bit too unsympathetically, I thought, I suspected that what she really meant was she'd be delighted to leave me behind).

'Of course I can,' I said. 'You go off and enjoy yourself, Tracy. You'll love the museum.'

'I won't,' Tracy sighed. 'I'm very sorry. My mother says I worry too much about other people, but that's just the way I am. I would be really miserable all the time we were there, and I wouldn't be able to concentrate on anything. Not when he's so ill.'

'We understand,' said Dad. 'That's one of the drawbacks of being a caring person. We'll all go together when he's feeling better.'

So, one point each, and although Tracy did well I still feel that I have the upper hand in this contest. After all, as I said before, this is my home ground and I haven't started to play my best game yet.

Sunday 3rd August
Curses! Today I was caught out.

You remember how I said that I had an

advantage because I was on my home ground, while Tracy was playing away from home? Well this is not the case! The cunning little flea-eared, locust-faced rat has turned the situation to her advantage by playing the part of the Visitor. This means that my parents can't order her about, while I am bullied and ordered about by them as if child slavery was still the order of the day.

To show you what I mean: this morning Mum and Dad came into the living room where I was watching television and Tracy was pretending to read a book, and announced, 'We've arranged for us all to visit your Aunt Maud today, Tracy. I know she'd love to see you while you're with us.'

Good, I thought. This is where I move into a 2–1 lead because I can get out of this easily. Aunt Maud has hated the sight of me ever since I played a joke on her over her budgie. Aunt Maud has this prize budgie she is very fond of, and its cage is in a place of honour in her kitchen, something I have personally always thought was very unhygienic. On this particular occasion, when Dad and Mum had taken me to visit, Aunt Maud had said to me, 'Would you like to feed little Herbert?' which was what she calls her budgie.

'Certainly, Auntie,' I said, and trotted off to the kitchen, where I rattled the cage and made a few budgie-like chirrups and a few miaows. Then I went back into the living room, where they all gave me a puzzled look that showed all those funny noises had worried them.

'Did you feed little Herbert?' Aunt Maud asked.

'Yes, Auntie,' I said. 'I fed him to the cat.'

I thought it was funny (it was supposed to be, anyway), but Aunt Maud thought I meant it and crashed to the floor in a dead faint. It took half an hour for Dad and Mum to revive her, by which time, naturally, I was well away to somewhere safe.

Anyway, since that day Aunt Maud has not been my greatest fan. Tracy, on the other hand, couldn't possibly get out of this visit easily.

I was just smirking to myself, when Tracy said: 'Oh I'd love to visit Aunt Maud, but I really don't think I ought to go.'

'Why ever not?' said Mum. 'Aunt Maud would love to see you.'

'And I would love to see Aunt Maud,' said Tracy, 'but it would be best if I didn't go to her house.'

'Why? What's wrong with her house?' I demanded, determined that Tracy wasn't going to get out of this visit easily.

'Nothing,' said Tracy, 'except little Herbert, her beautiful little budgerigar. If I go there I may kill it.'

Well, I could understand that. The way Aunt Maud dotes on it is sickening. It is spoiled something rotten, and I have often been tempted to give it a punch in the beak just to bring it down a peg or two, but I thought Tracy was being a bit rash admitting it out loud.

'Kill it?' said Dad.

'Yes,' said Tracy. 'You see, our doctor discovered that I'm a carrier of a budgerigar disease known as wing croup, which can be fatal to the dear little birds.'

At the sight of Mum's face, obviously wondering whether she ought to disinfect everywhere in the house, Tracy added quickly, 'It doesn't affect humans at all. Or any other animals. Only budgies. It's very rare, but I'd hate to pass it on to little Herbert and be the cause of his death. I could never forgive myself. And it would upset poor Aunt Maud.'

It could also upset my chances of winning our bet. Aloud I said: 'I've never heard of wing croup. Why don't we phone Aunt Maud and see what she says?'

'I don't think that would be right,' said Tracy. 'It wouldn't be fair to alarm her. Far better to tell her I've got a cold, but that I'll see her in a few days when I'm better. Then maybe she could come here.'

'Yes, I can see that,' said Dad, nodding. 'It's a pity, though, Aunt Maud's expecting us and she'll have prepared a special tea.'

'There's no reason you three can't go,' said Tracy sweetly. 'I'll be perfectly all right on my own. You won't be long, and this really is an interesting book I'm reading.'

'Well, if you're sure you don't mind,' said Dad.

'I mind!' I pointed out.

'Tough,' said Mum. 'I'm not letting Aunt Maud down by not turning up at all.'

'Then you go and I'll stay here and look after Tracy,' I said.

'I wouldn't trust you to look after King Kong,' said Mum. 'You're going whether you like it or not. Get your anorak on.'

And that was that. No further discussion, no voting, just me forced into my anorak and whisked out of the front door. I am living in a dictatorship!

Mind, I had my own back when we got there. I put a few drops of Aunt Maud's gin in little Herbert's water and he fell off his perch, paralytic drunk, flat on his back on the floor of his cage with his feet in the air.

Once more Maud had a fainting fit, and hopefully I'm banned from going there for a good few months.

Still, the score stands at 2–1 to Tracy!

I just can't believe it. This horrible little worm is going to be a tougher opponent than I thought.

Monday 4th August

Tracy is a liar and a cheat and everything rotten! Today she moved into a two point lead, and she did it by A Lie!

Mum said that she was going to give us a treat and take us to the pictures. Now we had already agreed that this counted as being OK. Mum said she wasn't telling us what she was going to take us to see because she wanted it to be a surprise for us when we arrived at the cinema. Our local cinema has five screens and I had checked in the local paper and found out that the five films on were: a horror film, a war film, a cartoon, a car chase comedy, and some boring film about ballet.

Tracy whispered to me that she'd overheard Mum tell Dad that she was taking us to see the car chase comedy. I said, 'Good, anything so long as it's not that boring ballet film.' And, of course, that's the film that Mum took us to see! And Tracy knew all along and had lied: (a) to get me into the cinema before I knew what film we were going to see; and (b) to get me to admit that I wouldn't want to see her rotten ballet film, so that she would get the point.

So it's 3–1 to Tracy, and my reputation as the world's greatest dodger is in real danger.

I shall have to do something drastic. I only have four days left to save the situation!

Tuesday 5th August

Today I clawed back a point. The score is now 3–2 to Tracy but I'm closing fast.

I was so angry at the way that Tracy had conned me over this ballet film yesterday that I decided it would be poetic justice to use the same method against her (but altered obviously, otherwise she'd be suspicious).

I told Mum that Tracy and I had been talking, and she had told me that her dearest wish while she was staying with us was to do some brass rubbings at the local church.

What Tracy had actually said to me was: 'A month ago my Mother took me on the most boring day out I've ever been on. We did brass rubbings. You put a big sheet of paper on a grave and you have to rub it with a crayon. I got it all over my dress and it never came off. I hated it. If anyone ever shows me a brass rubbing again I shall vomit all over it.' (See, I knew she could be sick at will and that last Christmas's vomiting incident hadn't been an accident.)

Anyway, so that Tracy wouldn't be able to get out of it, I told Mum not to tell Tracy where she was taking her. 'Tell her you're taking her to buy another frilly dress. Then she'll get such a wonderful surprise when she finds herself doing a brass rubbing.'

And that was how I used Tracy's own method against her. Fortunately Mum didn't want me coming with her and Tracy, mainly because I've not been very popular at our local church since I offered to help at a service and I charged people 25p each to hire a hymn book. As a result of that I was condemned from the pulpit by the vicar and my parents claimed that they could 'never hold up our heads in public again'.

The end result of today: Tracy came back with crayon and other stains all over her dress. According to Mum, 'poor Tracy' had been taken

ill as soon as the brass rubbing started, and she had thrown up over it.

'Oh dear, oh dear,' I said. 'What a pity. Poor Tracy.'

Tracy looked at me, and if looks could have killed I'd have been dead on the spot.

I shall have to watch my step tomorrow and the next few days. Tracy is going to be after me with a vengeance.

Wednesday 6th August
Three—all!

As I expected, Tracy tried to get her own back on me today, but it backfired on her.

She was so annoyed over the brass rubbings yesterday that she told my Dad and Mum that I had been showing an interest in ancient buildings, and asked if we could both go to a talk that some idiot was giving on old buildings in our town this evening. How my parents even fell for this garbage is beyond belief. Surely they have known me long enough to know that I would never even be seen dead at such a talk! But they did fall for it, and this evening we were told to get ready for a 'wonderful' evening sitting in a draughty room at the back of the Town Hall, while this local idiot showed us slides of these really boring, uninteresting buildings.

However, I expected that Tracy would have something up her sleeve, so I was prepared.

'Wonderful!' I said with lots of enthusiasm. 'This is the talk that Tracy was telling me about earlier. We've both been really looking forward to it. I'm so glad we're going, aren't you, Tracy?'

This put her on the spot and forced her (through gritted teeth) to say that she was delighted to be going.

'But first I've just got to pop round to my friend John and lend him a history book,' I said. 'He needs it for his homework.'

Immediately Tracy saw through my plan.

'That's all right,' she said. 'We don't mind waiting until you come back from your friend's. Then we can all go together.'

'No no,' I said. 'You all go on first. That way we can make sure we get good seats in the front row. Save a chair for me and I'll be with you before it starts.'

Too late Tracy saw that her 'enthusiasm' for

this boring talk had sunk her. She had to grin and put up with it as she was being marched off to the Town Hall by Mum and Dad.

Needless to say, I never turned up. When they came back I gave them an excuse in three parts:

1. I couldn't find my history book at first.
2. John wasn't sure which part of the history book we had to work from, so I spent valuable time showing him (because I am such a wonderful bloke).
3. Because of my above unselfish act, I was late arriving at the Town Hall, and the attendant wouldn't let me in because the talk had already started. This had bitterly disappointed me.

It also bitterly disappointed Tracy. We were now on level points. One more point, and the genius to hang on to that lead, and victory (and the money) will be mine!

Thursday 7th August
Another visit to an ancient and boring relative lined up for us today, and all because of Tracy. What I cannot understand is why I have to be involved? If these idiotic relatives insist on having the human frog inflicted on them for tea, why do I have to be dragged along? Why must I suffer as well?

The relative today was my (and Tracy's) Grandad (on my Dad's side), who is enough to drive anyone mad.

He was an Air Raid Warden in the tiny village of Little Something-or-Other somewhere in East

Anglia during the Second World War. From what I can gather from other people all he ever did was wear a tin hat and walk around at night shining a torch into dark corners and telling people to turn their lights out. The fact that he was the one lighting everything up with his torch never seemed to occur to him. Also, in the whole course of the war only one bomb fell on this village, and that was dropped accidentally by a British plane. Luckily it never went off, it just fell on the local pub and demolished the roof.

So, as I say, Grandad didn't exactly have a huge part to play in the War. Unless you hear him talk about it, that is. The way that Grandad tells it, he won the whole war single-handed. According to him the Prime Minister used to phone him up and ask him how things were going, and he was always keeping battalions of fully-armed Gestapo at bay with just a shotgun and a catapult.

Anyway, Tracy and I realized there was very little either of us could do to get out of being dragged along to Grandad's. (An invitation to Grandad's house is like a Royal Command, you can only get out of it if you're dead. And even then they'd have to take your coffin along so he could check you weren't making excuses.) So we resigned ourselves to being taken, but resolved to make sure that we were never invited back again.

We agreed that we both had to do our best to make sure that we weren't invited back if we were to get a point each. I thought this was a good idea, because I couldn't imagine Tracy being badly behaved in Grandad's house, so I felt sure of winning the point and establishing a one-point lead. However, I hadn't reckoned on just how determined not to lose she was.

I have to admit, she did upset him (and my Mum and Dad) in a very subtle way by sweetly and angelically asking him embarrassing questions about his war service. It went a bit like this:

Tracy: 'Grandpa!'
Grandpa: 'Yes, Tracy?'

Tracy: 'How many Germans did you capture in the War?'

Grandpa: (*Modestly*) 'On my own, about a dozen. Although with my unit (*The Battalion of Air Raid Wardens?*) we must have captured between fifty and a hundred.'

Tracy: 'That's odd.'

Grandpa: 'What is?'

Tracy: 'Well my teacher at school was brought up in the same village, and he told us in history that no German was ever there in either of the two World Wars.' (*Here she gave an angelic simper.*) 'If you tell me when it all happened I'll be able to tell him he's wrong.'

At this there was one of those wonderful embarrassed silences as everyone coughed and tried to pretend that something else was happening. Grandad tried to cover it by claiming that it must have been another Little Something-or-Other that this teacher was talking about, but Tracy came back with: 'Oh no, it's definitely the same one, because he was a boy then and he remembers you were the Air Raid Warden. Don't you think it's funny that he can't remember the German prisoners you captured? Shall I bring him round to see you?'

She also, with the same sweet smile, suggested that he had spent the war either drunk at the local pub, or hiding in barns. It was a brilliant performance and she deserved her point. I had never seen Grandad look so angry, or Dad and Mum look so embarrassed.

I earned my point by making remarks about his personal freshness:

Me: Cor, Grandad, is that pong coming from you? Has your water been turned off?' and similar things.

Grandad was so upset at Tracy's demolition of his War Hero status, and because I wasn't as subtle, that he simply growled, 'That boy needs a good clip round the ear.' He also refused to give me the fifty pence he usually gives me when I visit.

Still, I got my point, so the score is still a draw at four points all.

Friday 8th August
At last! Tracy's last day here, and I did it! I just pipped her at the post in the last round and got that winning point!

This evening Dad and Mum suddenly sprang on us both that as it was Tracy's last night with us they were going to take us out for an evening's entertainment. At first we both felt quite pleased. The pictures? After all, we wouldn't be going to see that rotten ballet film again. But no, Dad had been given tickets to a violin recital in the local church hall. Argh! No wonder he was given the tickets. I bet they were offering people pound notes if they'd take a bunch. If there is one thing I cannot abide it is the sound of someone scraping a violin; it sounds like a cat having teeth out. I could see from Tracy's face that she felt the same way, and an idea struck me.

After tea I grabbed her on her own and whispered: 'Well, it looks as if we're caught. It's not going to be easy getting out of this, not as they're taking us out for a special occasion for your last night here. As it's a draw already, why don't we accept it? At least then neither of us loses our money.'

'I suppose so,' she sighed. 'Still, it was a good contest.'

'Come on you two!' called Dad. 'Get your coats on! The recital starts in just over half an hour.'

Tracy and I sighed in resignation and trudged upstairs to get our coats. I let Tracy go back down the stairs first (in fact I let her reach the bottom first), and then I pretended to trip at the top of the stairs, and tumbled all the way down to the bottom.

Yes, it was dangerous and in ordinary circumstances it would have taken a lot to get me to do something like that. But these were not ordinary circumstances. It wasn't the money (I'd want a lot more than five pounds to fall downstairs); it was my pride and my reputation. I could not allow myself to be beaten by this overdressed Sindy doll. And to have drawn with her would have been to lose. There can be only one winner in a game, and in this game it was going to be me.

I thought I saw a look of awe on her face as I lay in a heap at the bottom of the stairs. I had certainly bruised myself enough to deserve it.

The outcome was that Mum took Tracy to the violin recital, and Dad stayed behind to practise his First Aid on me. I ended up almost disappearing as he enthusiastically stuck plasters all over me and tied me up with bandages. But the main thing was: I had won!

Saturday 9th August

I cannot believe it! I have been conned by that fiend in human shape, that walking fancily dressed lump of bird droppings!

Tracy's parents came and collected her this morning, and as soon as she was gone I went along to the corner shop to pick up the envelope with my winnings from old Mr Carstairs.

I had been expecting some kind of double-cross from Tracy because these last few days have shown me what a cheat and a liar she is. Because of that I had made Mr Carstairs promise not to hand over the envelope to Tracy unless I was with her. This was because I suspected that Tracy might be underhanded enough to forge a note in my name saying he could hand the envelope over to her. (As a safety precaution, I had already forged a note in her name in case it was necessary to get my five pounds back.)

Because I had taken these precautions I thought my money was safe, so you can imagine my shock and horror when I picked up the envelope from Mr Carstairs and opened it. Instead of finding two five pound notes inside it, I found a note from Tracy that read:

Dear Cousin. Well, I won. After all, the bet was to see who was the best dodger, and I have dodged you out of five pounds. I did it by switching the envelope with the money in for this one before we left the house, so I've had the money all the time. By the time you read this I will have spent it.

Better luck next time. Your cousin, Tracy.

I ask you! How low! How despicable! How rotten! What a cheat and a liar and everything rotten and horrible in the world that cousin of mine is!

The worst of it is that I daren't tell anybody the way she cheated me in order to get my money back, because to do so would ruin my reputation as the world's greatest dodger.

I am feeling too sick to write any more. I have been made to look an idiot! I shall have my own back, though. I shall get my parents to take me to visit Tracy and her family, and then watch out!